johnny me

C000242005

contents

11	AC-CENT-TCHU-ATE THE POSITIVE
2	AND THE ANGELS SING
6	BLUES IN THE NIGHT
16	COME RAIN OR COME SHINE
20	DAY IN, DAY OUT
25	DREAM
28	FOOLS RUSH IN (WHERE ANGELS FEAR TO TREAD)
32	GOODY GOODY
40	I THOUGHT ABOUT YOU
37	I WANNA BE AROUND
44	I'M OLD FASHIONED
52	JEEPERS CREEPERS
49	LAURA
58	LAZYBONES
68	MY SHINING HOUR
63	ONE FOR MY BABY (AND ONE MORE FOR THE ROAD)
72	SKYLARK
92	SOMETHING'S GOTTA GIVE
76	SUMMER WIND
80	TANGERINE
84	TOO MARVELOUS FOR WORDS
88	WHEN THE WORLD WAS YOUNG

Photograph by William P. Gottlieb

ISBN 978-1-4803-6238-3

HAL•LEONARD® CORPORATION

7777 W. BLUEMOUND RD. P.O. BOX 13819 MILWAUKEE, WI 53213

Visit Hal Leonard Online at
www.halleonard.com

AND THE ANGELS SING

Lyrics by JOHNNY MERCER
Music by ZIGGY ELMAN

Moderately slow, with rubato

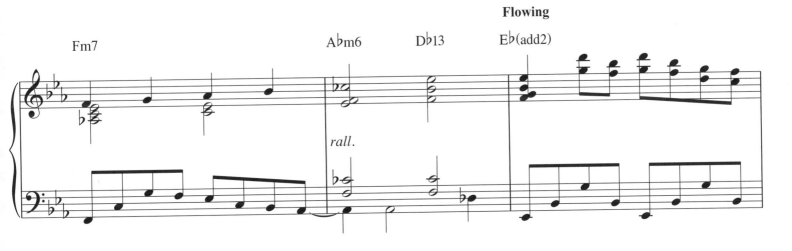

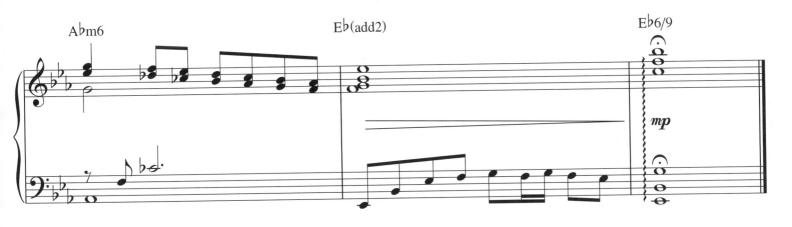

BLUES IN THE NIGHT

Words by JOHNNY MERCER
Music by HAROLD ARLEN

AC-CENT-TCHU-ATE THE POSITIVE

from the Motion Picture HERE COME THE WAVES

Lyric by JOHNNY MERCER
Music by HAROLD ARLEN

COME RAIN OR COME SHINE
from ST. LOUIS WOMAN

Words by JOHNNY MERCER
Music by HAROLD ARLEN

DAY IN, DAY OUT

Words by JOHNNY MERCER
Music by RUBE BLOOM

DREAM

Words and Music by
JOHNNY MERCER

FOOLS RUSH IN
(Where Angels Fear to Tread)

Lyrics by JOHNNY MERCER
Music by RUBE BLOOM

Moderately slow, with expression

GOODY GOODY

Words by JOHNNY MERCER
Music by MATT MALNECK

Bright Swing

I WANNA BE AROUND

Words by JOHNNY MERCER
Music by SADIE VIMMERSTEDT

Slowly, with feeling

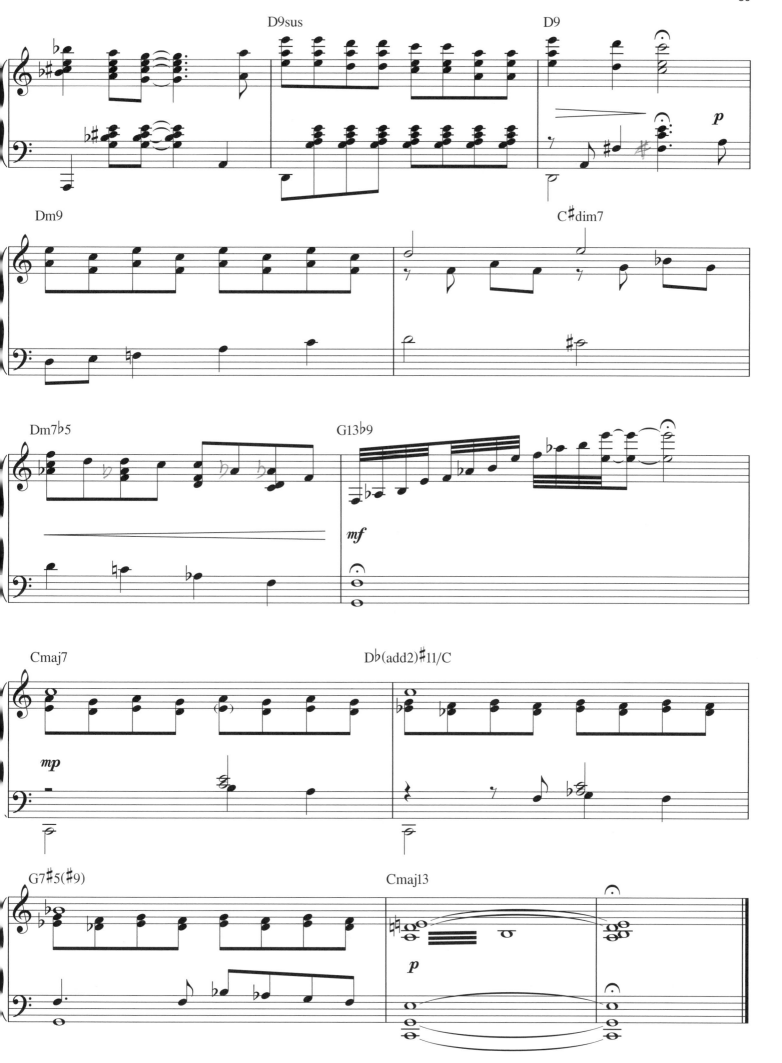

I THOUGHT ABOUT YOU

Words by JOHNNY MERCER
Music by JIMMY VAN HEUSEN

I'M OLD FASHIONED
from YOU WERE NEVER LOVELIER

Lyrics by JOHNNY MERCER
Music by JEROME KERN

Bright Swing

Arrangement based on one by Oscar Peterson

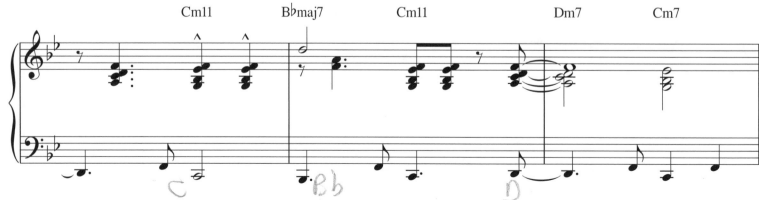

LAURA
from LAURA

Lyrics by JOHNNY MERCER
Music by DAVID RAKSIN

Slowly, with expression

JEEPERS CREEPERS

Words by JOHNNY MERCER
Music by HARRY WARREN

Bright Swing

55

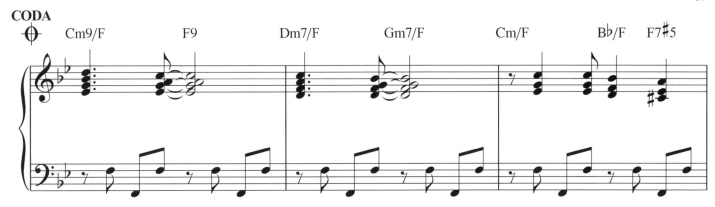

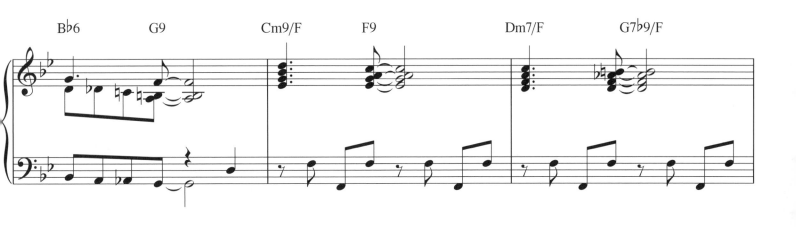

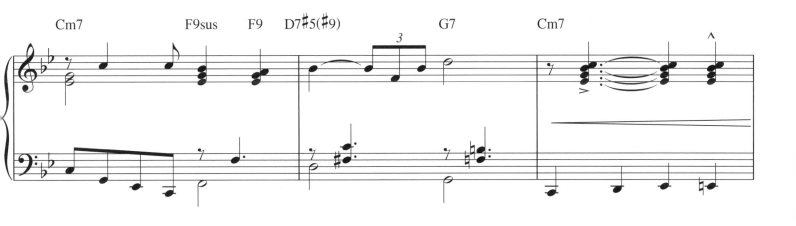

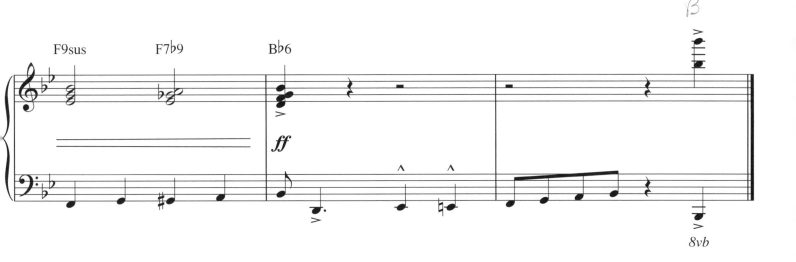

LAZYBONES

Words and Music by HOAGY CARMICHAEL
and JOHNNY MERCER

Slow Blues

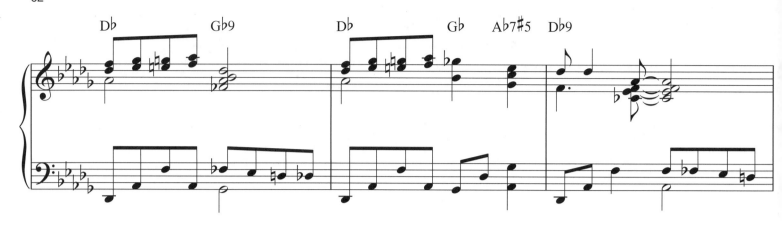

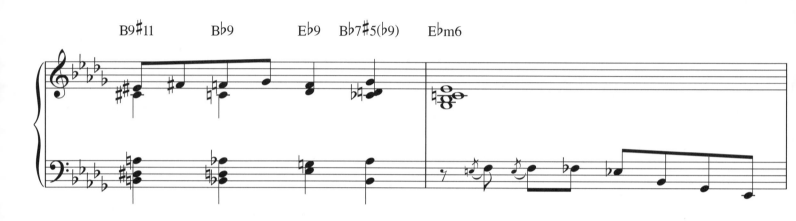

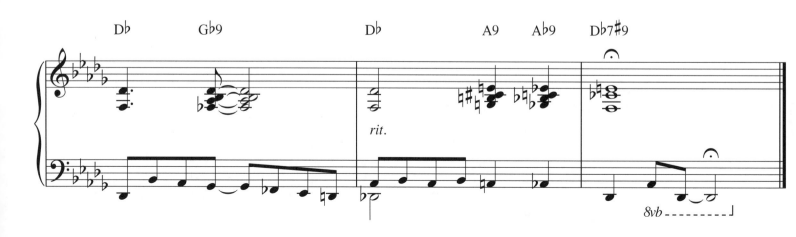

ONE FOR MY BABY
(And One More for the Road)
from the Motion Picture THE SKY'S THE LIMIT

Lyric by JOHNNY MERCER
Music by HAROLD ARLEN

MY SHINING HOUR
from the Motion Picture THE SKY'S THE LIMIT

Lyric by Johnny Mercer
Music by Harold Arlen

SKYLARK

Words by JOHNNY MERCER
Music by HOAGY CARMICHAEL

SUMMER WIND

English Words by JOHNNY MERCER
Original German Lyrics by HANS BRADTKE
Music by HENRY MAYER

Easy Latin groove

TANGERINE
from the Paramount Picture THE FLEET'S IN

Words by JOHNNY MERCER
Music by VICTOR SCHERTZINGER

Moderate Latin groove

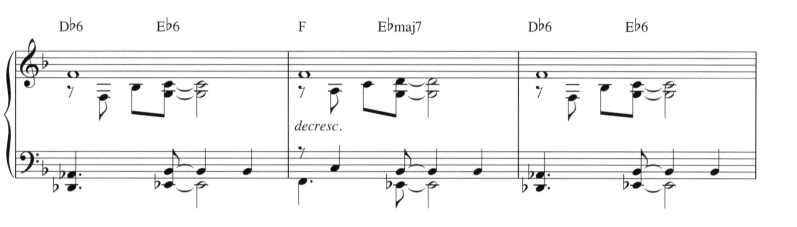

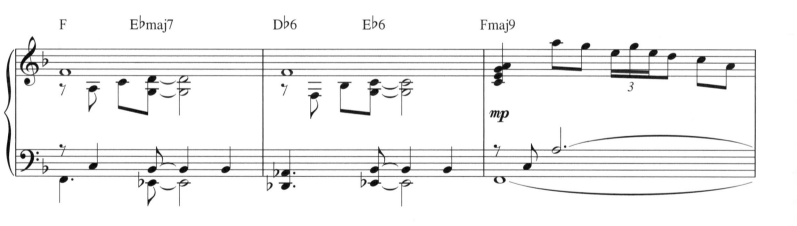

TOO MARVELOUS FOR WORDS

Words by JOHNNY MERCER
Music by RICHARD A. WHITING

Whimsically

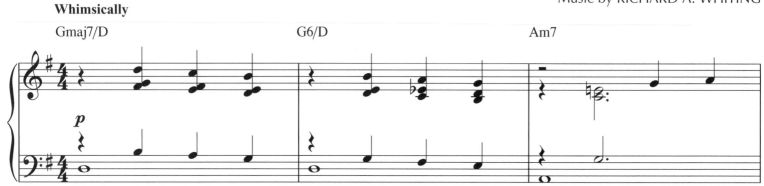

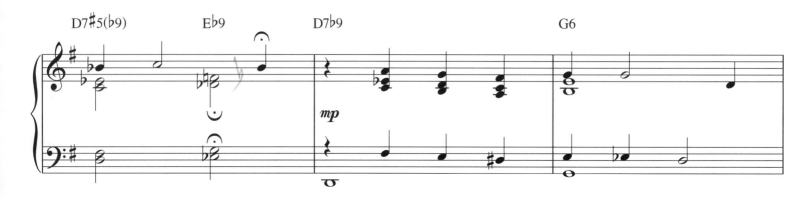

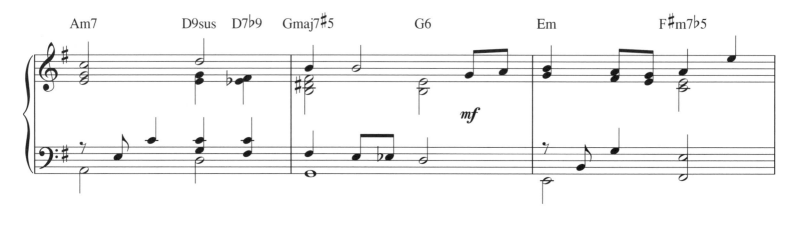

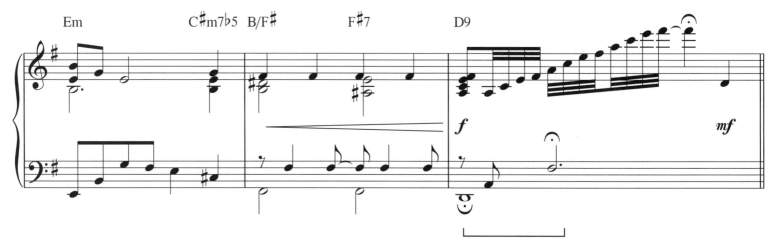

WHEN THE WORLD WAS YOUNG

English Lyric by JOHNNY MERCER
French Lyric by ANGELE VANNIER
Music by M. PHILIPPE-GERARD

SOMETHING'S GOTTA GIVE
from DADDY LONG LEGS

Words and Music by
JOHNNY MERCER

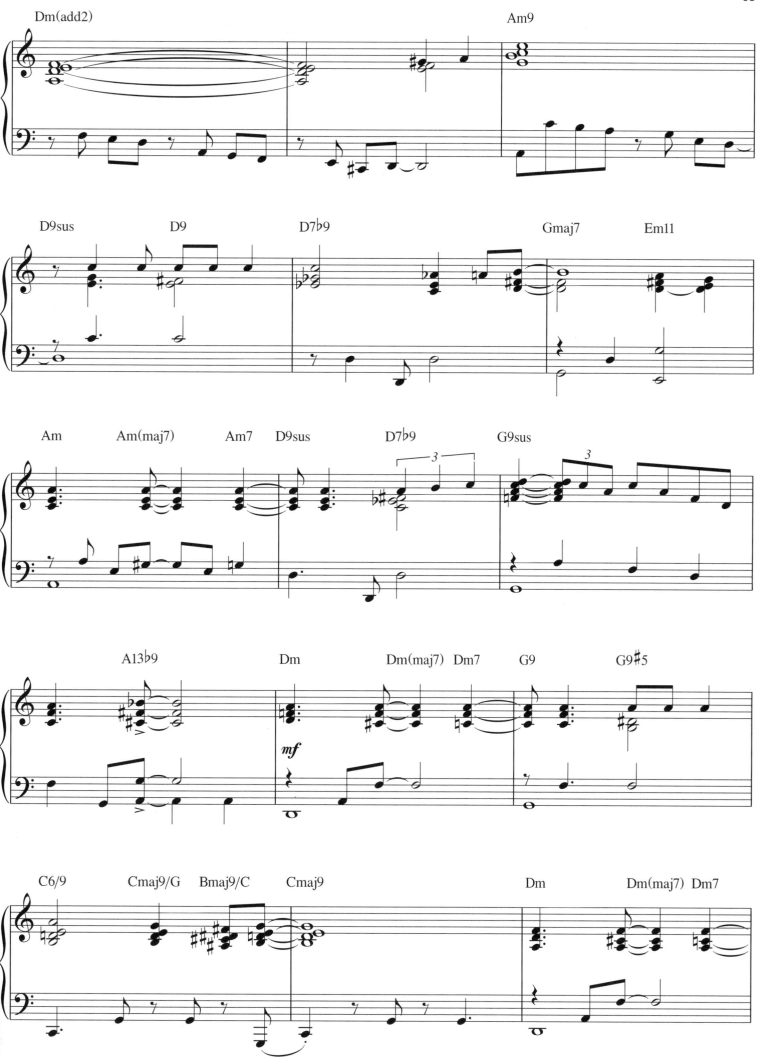